Q&A

The
Buddha

LIFE AND THEMES
563 BC
483 BC

...off the record

Q&A

The Buddha

LIFE AND THEMES
563 BC
483 BC

...off the record

JOAN DUNCAN OLIVER

Foreword by
ANNIE LENNOX

WATKINS PUBLISHING

LONDON

The Buddha
Joan Duncan Oliver

This edition first published in the United Kingdom and Ireland in 2010
by Watkins Publishing, an imprint of Duncan Baird Publishers Ltd
Sixth Floor, Castle House
75–76 Wells Street, London W1T 3QH

Conceived, created and designed by Duncan Baird Publishers

Co-ordinating Editors: Daphne Razazan and James Hodgson
Assistant Editor: Kirty Topiwala
Managing Designer: Clare Thorpe

British Library Cataloguing-in-Publication Data:
A CIP record for this book is available from the British Library

ISBN: 978-1-907486-60-9

10 9 8 7 6 5 4 3 2 1

Typeset in Dante MT and Baskerville BT
Printed in Shanghai by Imago

Publisher's note:
The interviews in this book are purely fictional, while being based
on Buddhist texts. They take place between a fictionalized Buddha
and an imaginary interviewer.

CONTENTS

FOREWORD by Annie Lennox

My first significant encounter with Buddhism was vivid and unforgettable. Years ago when I was a student in London, a friend took me to see a group of Tibetan monks chanting and playing traditional ceremonial instruments. I was fascinated by the cacophonous sounds of clashing cymbals juxtaposed against high-pitched wind instruments (like oboes gone mad), all underscored by a backwash of primordial sound. To top it all, the monks were wearing a fabulous combination of medieval-style maroon robes, set off with yellow pointed headgear. I felt I'd encountered something ancient and mystical, even though I had little clue as to the ritualistic meaning of what was going on.

I've always been drawn to "otherness." The idea of a Buddhist monk or nun sitting for hours in seated meditation has always intrigued me. At first my response was, Why on earth would anyone want to do that? Later on I think I began to understand it a little better.

I wasn't brought up in any particular religion or spiritual tradition, and I believe this was an advantage in a certain way. I have always felt free to explore possibilities, without being too much encumbered by those terrible burdens of dogmatically informed fear and guilt that have so badly affected many people.

Eastern literature attracted me. I came across the poems of the Chinese poet Lao Tzu in meta-physical bookstores. I looked at Zen texts too—the koans and haiku. I wondered if by any chance I might discover the "meaning of existence" through the combination of words laid out succinctly but obscurely before me.

Over the years I've chosen much of my reading material from the great Buddhist communicators— people like His Holiness the Dalai Lama, Chögyam Trungpa Rinpoche, and Pema Chödrön, among many others. I like to think of myself as being open to wisdom wherever I find it, rather than attaching myself to a particular group or sect—although I've had a few close encounters along the way. I'm wary of the cult of personality surrounding many teachers and gurus; on the other hand, I recognize that a charismatic teacher is, for many, an essential part of their development.

We can all aspire to embracing peace and love, but in this world of temporary and unpredictable existence what we often engender instead is a state of constant fearfulness. No matter how we direct our energies, we can't escape suffering in one form or another. Our desires bring no contentment, even when they're fulfilled. Buddhism can offer

ways of dealing with all this. Compassion being
the fundamental key.

When things get dark, and hard to handle,
Buddhist philosophy can be inspirational—with
a simple reminder to breathe, to go easy on the
day, moment by moment, to be mindful if we can.
As Pema Chödrön so succinctly put it, Buddhism
offers us the option of learning how to be
"comfortable with the notion of insecurity."

Annie Lennox

INTRODUCTION

We know him as the Buddha, the "Awakened One," one of the world's greatest spiritual leaders. He wasn't a god but an ordinary mortal—born Siddhartha Gautama 2,500 years ago in northern India. His humanity speaks to us today. He suffered as we do, then by his own efforts found the key to liberation from the bonds of desire, hatred, and ignorance. As Westerners living in relative prosperity, we can identify with this man who had it all—love, success, money, talent, privilege—but set it aside to search for something deeper and more enduring.

How did he do it? What did he learn? If the Buddha were here now, how might he explain the truths he uncovered? Sit down with these pages and for the next hour or so, the Buddha's wisdom is yours for the asking.

THE BUDDHA (c.563–c.483BC)

His Life in Short

The earth trembles. Lions and tigers, serpents and scorpions grow tame. Diseases fall away from the sick. Humans shower one another with kindness. Such marvels herald a wondrous event: the birth of Siddhartha Gautama, who became the spiritual teacher known as the Buddha.

Legend has it that Mahamaya, Siddhartha's mother, was forewarned she would give birth to a *mahapurusha*, a great man. In a dream, she was transported by heavenly spirits to a plateau high in the Himalayas, where a magnificent white elephant pierced her side with its tusk and entered her womb. The dream, interpreted by Brahmin priests, prepared her for the arrival of a hero.

The child was born not in the city of Kapilavastu, where Mahamaya lived with her husband, Suddhodana, ruler of the Sakya clan, but in a grove of trees in the park at nearby Lumbini. Choosing the noblest tree, Mahamaya grasped a branch for support and gave birth painlessly, standing up. It is said that the newborn sprang to his feet, took seven strides, and surveying the four directions, cried: "I am born for enlightenment for the good of the world." Her sacred task complete, Mahamaya died within the week. The child's care fell to her sister, Mahapajapati, Suddhodana's second wife.

Word of the birth spread quickly. The seer Asita rushed to the infant's side and saw that he bore the thirty-two auspicious marks of a *mahapurusha*, among them the imprint of a wheel on the sole of each foot. "This one is unsurpassed," Asita said. With tears in his eyes he prophesied, "This prince will touch the ultimate self-awakening. He ... will set the wheel of dharma rolling out of compassion for all."

Suddhodana and Mahamaya named their son Siddhartha—"he who accomplishes." Brahmin priests predicted the boy would become either a "world-turning" monarch—a *chakravartin*—or a Buddha, an "awakened one." One priest said that if Siddhartha saw four things—a sick man, an old man, a dead man, and a monk—then he would renounce worldly existence for a holy life.

The Four Sights

Suddhodana was determined to keep his son on the universal-monarch track. He filled Siddhartha's life with every possible delight, shielding him from misery of any kind. "I lived in … total refinement," the Buddha later said of his youth. "A white sunshade was held over me day and night to protect me from cold, heat, dust, dirt, and dew."

Siddhartha had at his disposal not one but three palaces—for the winter, summer, and rainy seasons. Talk, dark-haired, and handsome, he possessed wealth and promise. But when it was time to wed, the parents of prospective brides were wary. How could anyone so pampered ever lead a kingdom? Chagrined, Suddhodana immersed his son in the warrior arts.

In one version of the tale, Siddhartha was given a giant bow to string—a feat that usually took several men. He not only strung the bow with ease but out-shot the other archers. Reassured of Siddhartha's prowess, the local gentry presented their daughters at the palace for his approval. As each young hopeful came forward, Siddhartha reached into a coffer of jewels and chose a bauble for her. Finally the last young woman stood before him. Alas, the chest was empty. The assembly held its breath. What would he do? Not missing a beat, Siddhartha took off his own emerald necklace and slipped it over the young woman's head. This was the lovely Yasodhara, who became his wife and bore him a son, Rahula.

Siddhartha's life was now complete, yet still he grew restless and yearned to taste the world. One day he persuaded his charioteer Chandra to drive him out beyond the palace gates. The gods decided it was time to set the future Buddha's destiny in motion. On entering Kapilavastu, Siddhartha spotted a gray-haired man. "What is this?" he asked Chandra. "Old age," he was told. "The murderer of beauty, the ruin of vigor, the birthplace of sorrow, the grave of pleasure …" "Quick, let's go home," Siddhartha said, but the seed was planted. "How can I take pleasure in the garden, when the fear of old age rules in my mind?" he lamented.

On another excursion, Siddhartha saw a sick man; on still another, a corpse. With each encounter, Siddhartha grew more despondent: "How this world has fallen on difficulty! People are born, they age, they die, and they're reborn, but they can't see how to escape from this suffering."

His fourth encounter was with a wandering monk. Siddhartha was riveted by his calm. "Who is that?" he asked Chandra. "A man who lives in utter simplicity, retired from the world," was the reply. Was this the answer? Living a holy life amid everyday distractions isn't easy, the Buddha later acknowledged. "The thought came to me, 'Suppose I shaved off my hair and beard, put on the yellow robe, and went forth … into homelessness?'" He was then twenty-nine.

Going Forth

A few nights later, after an evening's entertainment, Siddhartha awoke to find the performers asleep, sprawled around the room, their mouths agape. The sight filled him with disgust. Didn't these women understand that youth and beauty are fleeting? Surely there was more to life than passing pleasures. It was time to "go forth" as a homeless seeker.

While Chandra saddled his horse, Siddartha went to the chamber where his wife and infant son lay sleeping. He intended to kiss Rahula goodbye, but when he saw he might also rouse Yasodhara, he tiptoed off. If she woke, he feared he would lose his resolve. Once he became a Buddha, he would come back and see his son.

Just as Siddhartha was about to leave the palace, he had his first run-in with Mara—the "Evil One" who would return to test him at key moments throughout his life. This was the voice of temptation—Siddhartha's still-deluded mind—urging him to stick to the familiar path rather than strike out on the hard road to enlightenment. If Siddhartha would just forget this silly renunciation idea and turn back to the palace, in seven days he would be a universal monarch, Mara promised. Siddhartha brushed him aside. "Big mistake," Mara countered. "From now on, I'll follow you like a shadow. You'll never be free of me."

When Siddhartha and Chandra reached the edge of the forest, Siddhartha handed the charioteer the reins of his horse and sent him back to the palace. Chandra begged to accompany his master, but to no avail. Later, Chandra became one of the Buddha's followers, but the horse, it is said, died of a broken heart that night.

Siddhartha cut off his hair and beard, and traded his sumptuous garments for the humble robe of a passerby. Now he was officially a wandering monk. One day, as Siddhartha visited the city of Rajagaha with his begging bowl, King Bimbisara, the local ruler, spotted the young monk. "You have the look of a warrior-noble, one fit to lead an army," Bimbisara told Siddhartha. "I offer you a fortune to lead mine."

"I haven't gone forth to seek the pleasures of the world," Siddhartha replied. "I see danger in them and seek refuge in a life of renunciation. That is my heart's desire." Disappointed, but impressed with the young man's sincerity, Bimbisara said, "When you find what you're looking for, return and teach me."

Tying the Air into Knots

In search of "the unexcelled state of sublime peace," Siddhartha cast about for a teacher. From one master, Alara Kalama, he learned advanced yogic techniques for transcending the mind to reach a state of "nothingness." At the feet of another, Uddaka Ramaputta, he attained an even higher state. But neither teacher knew the way to extinguish fear and desire and gain release from suffering. Siddhartha realized he would have to find that for himself.

Joining up with five ascetics, he spent the next six years in harsh, austere practices to subdue body and mind, fasting until he was so emaciated he could feel his backbone when he touched his belly. Such extreme self-mortification increased his *siddhis*—clairvoyance and other supranormal powers—but brought him no closer to nirvana. Later the Buddha said this period was "like time spent trying to tie the air into knots."

One day, when Siddhartha had collapsed from hunger and exhaustion, Mara reappeared. "You poor thing, so close to death," he crooned. "Why don't you go home and be a compassionate world ruler instead?" Again, Siddhartha resisted. Still, he couldn't deny that his way wasn't working. Something had to change.

His mind drifted back to an afternoon in childhood when his nursemaids had parked him in the shade of a rose-apple tree during a ploughing festival. When they returned, they found Siddhartha seated cross-legged in meditation. He could still recall the feeling of happiness and well-being that had spontaneously welled up in him that day. Could that, rather than "grueling penance," be the key to awakening? Clearly he couldn't find bliss on an empty stomach. He decided to break his fast. Legend has it that just at that moment a young girl came by and offered him a bowl of rice milk.

The Great Awakening

His strength restored, Siddhartha renewed his push for enlightenment. The five ascetics had deserted him, thinking he had "given up the struggle and reverted to luxury." Never mind. He had more important things to do. On the bank of the Neranjara River, where the town of Bodhgaya now stands, Siddhartha selected a pipal tree—later called the Bodhi, or Buddha tree— and sat down under it, vowing not to move until he had attained nirvana.

An essential part of Buddhist mythology is that his great awakening took place over the course of one eventful night. But first Siddhartha had to contend with his old nemesis Mara. Once again the Evil One tried to deflect him from his goal. Mara stirred up a whirlwind and fired off a barrage of spears and arrows, but Siddhartha remained unmoved. Enraged, Mara unleashed his army of demons, but they too were repelled. "Desire, discontent, laziness, fear, indecision, criticism of others—these are your armies," said Siddhartha. "A lazy, cowardly person cannot overcome them, but I will destroy them with wisdom."

Mara pulled out his last card. "Get up, Siddhartha," he boomed. "That seat belongs to me." "No, Mara," Siddhartha replied. This was the seat all Buddhas-to-be had occupied in attaining enlightenment, he said. It belongs to the one whose "purpose is to deliver all creation from the snares of delusion. It does not befit you," Siddhartha continued, "to try and kill someone who is exerting himself to free humanity from their bondage."

"But who will bear witness to your efforts?" Mara sneered. Siddhartha reached down and touched the ground. The earth gave a thunderous shudder of support. Defeated, Mara withdrew.

His inner demons subdued, Siddhartha entered into deep meditation, passing through the four *jnanas*, or states of absorption, until his mind was calm and clear. Then, one by one, his former lifetimes passed before his eyes. Watching them come and go, he grasped the truth of impermanence as an essential factor of existence. Everything that arises passes away.

Siddhartha's second awareness was the truth of karma, the law of action. Surveying the thirty-one realms of existence, he saw that all beings are reborn in accord with their past actions. Bad conduct leads to an unhappy rebirth, good conduct to a happy one.

Then, in the final hours of the night, Siddhartha had his most profound awareness—the fundamental laws of existence he later called the Four Noble Truths. He understood the truth of *dukkha*, the basic suffering or dissatisfaction of life: "Birth is suffering, aging is suffering, sorrow and lamentation, pain, grief, and despair are suffering." He saw, too, the cause of *dukkha*—ignorance of the true nature of reality, and insatiable desire—and the cure: freedom from craving and self-grasping. Finally, he saw the means of awakening: the Noble Eightfold Path—the cultivation of morality, meditation, and wisdom.

As the morning star rose, Siddhartha attained nirvana—"aging-less, illness-less, deathless, sorrow-less, unexcelled rest from the yoke." The *bodhisattva*, the seeker of enlightenment, ceased to exist. In his place sat the Buddha, the Awakened One. Henceforth, he would be known as the Tathagatha, or "thus gone"—he was no longer caught in *samsara*, the cycle of death and rebirth. This lifetime would be his last.

After the Enlightenment

We are told the Buddha spent the next forty-nine days meditating near the Bodhi tree and further elaborating the profound truths he had struggled for so long to see. He began to wonder if he should teach them to others. No, he concluded, why bother? It would just be wasted words. This Dharma—this knowledge—was too subtle, too complex for most people to grasp.

At this point, the god Brahma Sahampati intervened. The human race was "drowning in pain," Brahma said. He begged the Buddha to reconsider. Realizing that his awakening was not for his benefit alone, the Buddha relented. But who would he tell first? His former teachers had died. Then he recalled the five ascetics, who were living in the Deer Park at Sarnath, near Benares (now Varanasi). He set off to find them. En route, the Buddha ran into another old pal from the forest. "Wow, you look terrific—so serene," the monk said. "Who's your teacher?" The Buddha described his great self-awakening but the monk was unconvinced. "Whatever," he muttered, shaking his head as he hurried off.

At first it looked as if the Buddha's reception at the Deer Park might be no better. Though the five ascetics were cordial, they hadn't forgotten that he'd "gone soft." Still, they too were drawn to the Buddha's serenity. After listening attentively as he explained the Four Noble Truths and the Middle Way—the path of moderation between self-indulgence and self-mortification—the ascetics were so inspired that soon all five were enlightened. They became the Buddha's first *bhikkus*, or monks.

Spreading the Dharma

The Buddha's sermon in the Deer Park—later known as "the first turning of the wheel of dharma"—marked the start of his 45-year teaching career. From then until his death at age 80, the Buddha crisscrossed the Ganges plain expounding the Dharma to monks, nuns, and "householders"—lay followers—of every stripe. The ten thousand or so *sutras*—texts relating the Buddha's teachings—that exist today reflect only a portion of the instruction he gave.

When sixty monks had attained enlightenment, the Buddha sent them out to spread the word. "Go now and wander for the welfare and the happiness of many, out of compassion for the world," he told them. "Teach the Dharma that is good in the beginning, good in the middle, and good in the end …" The *sangha*—the community of disciples—grew exponentially. For much of the year, the monks were itinerant, but during the rainy season they stayed in parks donated by wealthy followers. One, the Bamboo Grove, was a gift of appreciation from King Bimbisara, after the Buddha made good on his promise to return and instruct him. The *sangha*'s most generous benefactor was a merchant known as Anathapindika—

"feeder of the poor"—who was so intent on procuring a peaceful place of retreat for the Buddha that he once paved an entire park with gold pieces so the owner, Prince Jeta, would agree to sell it.

One by one, the Buddha's family joined the *sangha*. His stepmother even lobbied for the establishment of an order of Buddhist nuns. The Buddha refused until his ever-compassionate attendant, his cousin Ananda, persuaded him it was the right thing to do. Though the Buddha made no distinction between men and women in the teachings, for monastics it was another matter. To this day, Buddhist nuns have stricter rules—and lower status—than monks.

When the Buddha finally returned home to Kapilavastu, seven years after his enlightenment, his wife urged little Rahula, "Go ask your father for your inheritance." The boy expected riches, but the Buddha offered him something more precious—the Dharma. Rahula became a novice monk.

Not many dads dole out the Dharma as fatherly advice, but over the years Rahula received his share. One time the Buddha told Rahula never to lie, even in jest. He counseled the boy to examine his thoughts, speech, and actions as he would look at his reflection in a mirror, always making sure they would bring no harm to himself or others. Another time, Rahula—by then eighteen—was collecting alms with the Buddha when he started daydreaming about what his life might have been like if his father had been a universal monarch and not a monk. The Buddha brought him up short by admonishing, "Any material form or thought or feeling, past or present, should be regarded as 'This is not mine, this is not what I am, this is not my self.'" Whatever happens in life, good or bad, Rahula should not take it to heart or react to it, the Buddha said. He offered the following instruction:

> *Practice loving-kindness to get rid of ill will.*
> *Practice compassion to get rid of cruelty. Practice*
> *sympathy to get rid of apathy. Practice equanimity*
> *to get rid of resentment. Practice contemplation*
> *of loathsomeness in the body to get rid of lust.*
> *Practice contemplation of impermanence to get*
> *rid of the conceit "I am." Practice mindfulness of*
> *breathing; for when that is maintained in being*
> *and well developing, it brings great fruit and many*
> *blessings.*

Given the Buddha's emphasis on meditation as a means to awakening, we might assume he spent nearly all of his time in solitary contemplation. Not so. Except during the rainy season, when he went on retreat, the Buddha was constantly on the go. His jam-packed schedule closely resembled the present Dalai Lama's. People were constantly dropping by for advice or direction, or just to be in his presence. In the morning, the Buddha went out to collect alms, alone or with his monks. When he was invited to someone's house for a meal, he offered teachings in return. During the day he usually gave instruction to the monks and held public assemblies. He might take a short break to bathe and meditate before it was time for private interviews. Even when he retired at day's end, the Buddha was far from idle. He is said to have slept only an hour a night. While meditating, he would cast his wisdom eye over the earth and heavens, searching out all those in need of help.

The Buddha's boundless compassion was legendary. He never passed judgment on others or belittled their beliefs. As a result, some of the most unlikely people became ardent followers. At one point, a fearsome murderer named Angulimala was waylaying travelers, killing them and cutting off their fingers, which he wore on a string around his neck. One day, Angulimala spotted the Buddha walking along the road and thought, "Mmmm. A monk alone. I'll kill him." Sneaking up behind the Buddha, he yelled, "Stop, monk!" The Buddha turned around and said, "I have stopped, Angulimala: I have once and for all cast off violence to all beings. Why don't you stop, too?" With that, Angulimala threw himself at the Buddha's feet and asked to be ordained. Though he became a good monk, many people couldn't forget Angulimala's past and refused him food when he went on an alms run. "You'll just have to bear up," the Buddha told him gently. "This is the karmic result of your past deeds."

Final Nirvana

As he neared eighty, the Buddha began putting his affairs in order and preparing the *sangha* to carry on after his death. He had been through challenging times, including dissent in the *sangha* and even attempts on his life by his ambitious cousin. His chief disciples, Sariputta and Moggallana, and others close to him had died. The faithful Ananda kept his life running smoothly, and Ananda's memory for every word the Buddha uttered would prove invaluable after the Buddha's death, during the council to formalize the teachings and the rules for the order. But meanwhile, Ananda was so unhinged at the thought of losing his beloved teacher that he failed to pick up on several broad hints that the Buddha, if asked, could "live out the age"—stick around until the end of that historical era. By the time Ananda begged him, it was too late.

In an unguarded moment, the Buddha received one last visit from Mara. "You're tired. Why not just pack it in and go to your final nirvana?" the Evil One purred. "Not until everything's squared away with the Order," the Buddha said. With Ananda he made the rounds of his followers, two old men trudging from town to town. One day, the Buddha ate a meal of tainted food and realized the end had come. In a grove of trees at Kusinara (now Kusinagar), he lay down on his right side in his characteristic "lion" posture and, with his monks gathered around him, passed into *parinirvana*— his final release. The Buddha's last words to the *sangha* were ones of encouragement: "All conditioned things are subject to decay. Strive on [toward awakening] with diligence."

The Buddha left instructions for his cremation and the dispersal of his ashes, which were to be enshrined as relics at various spots. Today, these are pilgrimage destinations, along with the places of his birth, his enlightenment, his first sermon, and his death.

The Buddha's Legacy

From the beginning, the Buddha urged his followers not to become attached to him but to rely instead on the Dharma: "Be islands unto yourselves, refuges unto yourselves, seeking no external refuge, with the Dharma as your island." In any case, there was no separation between the two. "He who sees me sees the Dharma, and whoever sees the Dharma sees me," the Buddha said. Even then, people should not simply take him—or any teacher—at his word: "Do not place blind trust in impressive personalities or in venerated gurus, but examine the issue for yourselves. When you know for yourselves that something is wholesome and beneficial, then you should accept it and put it into practice." Ultimately, even the teachings had to be set aside, once they had served their purpose. Think of the Dharma as a raft, the Buddha said. You use it to transport yourself across the river, but when you're safely on the other shore, you set it down—you don't carry it with you. After you've reached nirvana, what need do you have for a raft?

The Buddha was, above all, a practical man. "I teach only suffering and the cessation of suffering," he often said. He refused to engage in speculative debate. Such discussions didn't facilitate awakening, he insisted. It's not that he didn't know the answers to metaphysical questions. In fact, he once grabbed a handful of leaves and told some monks that what he taught them was like the number of leaves in that handful, while what he knew was as vast as the number of leaves in the entire forest. Still, it was hard for some people to grasp the wisdom behind his unwillingness to philosophize. In one famous exchange, a man named Malunkyaputta refused to become a monk unless the Buddha explained his position on such questions as "Is the cosmos infinite?" The Buddha said Malunkyaputta was like someone who's been wounded with a poisoned arrow but won't let anyone remove it until he finds out the type of bow and arrow that struck him, the kind of poison, and the name and village of the archer. Metaphysical views cannot put an end to suffering, however.

The Buddha was adept at tailoring his teachings so that people at every level of awareness could benefit. He compared the Dharma to rain falling on grasses and trees: the rain's the same but each plant absorbs the amount it needs for growth. He used whatever means would help an individual awaken. One example he gave was the parable of a rich man whose house is burning. His children, oblivious to the danger, continue to play inside, refusing to leave. Finally, the father lures them to safety with the promise of wonderful toys awaiting them outside. *Upaya-kausalya*—"skill in means"— later became a key tenet of Mahayana Buddhism, the "second turning of the wheel of dharma."

Following the Buddha's death, Buddhism spread south to Sri Lanka and other parts of southern Asia. Then, with the rise of Mahayana teachings ("the Great Vehicle"), Buddhism migrated to East Asia and the Himalayas in the north. Today, the southern school is represented by Theravada Buddhism— "the Teachings of the Elders"—while the Mayahana tradition is represented largely by Chan/Zen and Tibetan Buddhism, or Vajrayana. The Vajrayana tradition evolved from Indian *tantra*, a mystical syncretism of Hindu and Buddhist beliefs. Sometimes called the "third turning of the wheel of dharma," Vajrayana emerged primarily in the Himalayan region and Mongolia. All three Buddhist traditions are now practiced in the West.

Q&A

NOW LET'S START TALKING ...

Over the following pages, the Buddha engages in
an imaginary conversation covering thirteen themes,
responding freely to searching questions.

The questions are in italic type;
the Buddha's answers are in roman type.

SUFFERING

LIFE IS HARD BUT HELP IS NEAR

Life is difficult, the Buddha said. Should we conclude, therefore, that pessimism is the only realistic view? Not at all. The Buddha acknowledged the struggles of ordinary life—we age, we get sick, and eventually we die; we don't get what we want, we get what we don't want, and even the good times pass. But he didn't leave it at that. The Four Noble Truths—the heart of the Buddha's teachings—not only diagnose the disease but proffer the cure. Followed diligently, the Noble Eightfold Path leads to nirvana and true happiness.

The essence of your teaching is contained in the Four Noble Truths. What's your message in a nutshell?

Suffering and the cessation of suffering.

That's all? Thousands of volumes of your words—and commentaries on your words—have appeared over the past 2,500 years, and that's your only message?

"Life is suffering but there is liberation from suffering." Is that more helpful?

"Life is suffering"—that's a pretty bleak assessment. No wonder people say Buddhism is pessimistic.

"Life is suffering" is neither pessimistic nor optimistic, it's realistic—a statement of the way things are. The Four Noble Truths aren't unremittingly bleak. Once these truths are deeply understood and the causes of suffering are removed, there's bliss beyond imagining—true happiness that isn't a result of getting or spending or other ephemeral pleasures.

That's promising. What are the Four Noble Truths?

The First Noble Truth is what we've been talking about: *Life is difficult. There is suffering.* The Pali

word for suffering is *dukkha*. It can mean physical
distress but more often it refers to mental anguish—
to the basic unsatisfactoriness of existence, to
the disappointment, frustration, and misery we
experience when we don't realize there's a better
way to live. What is suffering? Birth is suffering.
Aging and death are suffering. Sorrow, grief, pain,
and despair are suffering. To want something and not
get it or to get what you don't want is suffering. In
short, the human personality, with its propensity for
clinging and attachment, brings suffering.

*But surely there's more to life than pain. What about the
good times?*

Nothing wrong with the good times. But do they
bring lasting satisfaction? Even the best of life can
lead to disappointment. Everything—good or bad—
eventually passes. Just as suffering is a fundamental
mark of existence, so too is impermanence. And
when conditions change, how do you feel then? Think
about your own experience: when things pass away,
how does that affect you?

*It makes me sad, even angry sometimes, I have to confess.
Especially when I lose someone or something I really
care about.*

What do you do then?

I hold tight to what I have left, and strive harder to get what I want.

But all that striving only increases your longing and the fear of loss. The Second Noble Truth locates the origin of suffering—desire. The Pali word is *tanha*, meaning "thirst." There's a grasping, insatiable quality to this sort of desire. Craving drives the pursuit of power, possessions, pleasure, status—whatever burnishes the ego. The other side of desire is aversion—pushing away what we *don't* want. Meanwhile, in our ignorance, we redouble our efforts to attain the very things that caused our suffering in the first place. Attachment to what is "endearing and alluring"—including life itself—binds you to the wheel of *samsara*, the endless cycle of death and rebirth that prolongs the suffering, lifetime after lifetime.

Earlier you mentioned "cessation of suffering." If craving is the disease, what's the cure?

That's the Third Noble Truth: There's an end to craving and an escape from suffering. It's called *nirvana*. Nirvana is not easy to describe. To those who haven't experienced it, it's beyond comprehension.

To those who have, it's beyond words. Nirvana is often translated as "blowing out"—the extinguishing of the fires of desire and aversion, and the annihilation of ignorance. Nirvana means freedom from obsessive self-concern and self-grasping, freedom from attachment to the notion that you have an enduring "self" or eternal soul. Nirvana is true happiness that brings inner peace.

That's pretty radical. How do we attain this state?

The Fourth Noble Truth sets out the way—the Noble Eightfold Path.

I've been meaning to ask—why "Noble"?

Noble in this sense means "worthy" or "exalted"—it refers to those who understand these truths, not to the truths themselves. The Noble Eightfold Path is a prescription for spiritual development consisting of eight steps or stages that support one another. They're organized around three themes: morality, meditation, and wisdom.

The cultivation of wisdom focuses on Right View and Right Intention. "Right" in this context doesn't mean the opposite of "wrong." Rather, it means "perfect" or "appropriate." A deep understanding

of the Four Noble Truths and the workings of
karma constitutes Right View. (We can explore
karma in another conversation.) Right Intention—
sometimes called Right Thought—prepares the
mind for liberation. The positive qualities of
desirelessness, good will, and compassion are
developed to counter desire, ill will, and thoughts
of harm—all impediments to awakening.

Morality, or ethical conduct, builds on those
positive qualities, fostering consideration for
others through Right Speech, Right Action, and
Right Livelihood. Here, virtuous behavior is
promoted both for its own sake and as a means to
purify the mind and heart—essential for awakening.
The directives include everything from avoiding
gossip and idle chatter, to refraining from killing,
stealing, and harmful sex, to keeping your nose
clean in business.

Meditation rounds out the list. The focus here
is establishing mental discipline, out of which
comes insight into the true nature of reality. Right
Effort summons up the energy and will to do the
inner work of transformation—to sit in meditation
and counter doubt and other distracting thoughts
by cultivating wholesome mind states. Right
Mindfulness is moment-to-moment presence,
developed through awareness of the body, feeling,

and the workings and content of the mind. Right
Concentration is one-pointed attention leading
to ever-higher stages of meditative absorption,
culminating in bliss.

IMPERMANENCE

THIS TOO SHALL PASS

Life is continually in flux, a stream of phenomena arising and passing away. Like suffering and non-self, impermanence is one of the three marks of existence revealed to the Buddha on the night of his enlightenment. He pointed out the pain and disappointment we inevitably experience if we cling to what can't last. Only *nirvana*—the unconditioned— escapes the inexorability of time. Impermanence isn't all bad, however. Without change, there would be no life, no growth, no opportunity for spiritual awakening.

Impermanence seems to be central to your teachings. Why is it such a big deal?

Impermanence, or *anicca* in Pali, is one of the three basic characteristics of *samsara*—the world as we know it. It's intimately entwined with the other two characteristics: *dukkha*, the truth of suffering, and *anatta*, or non-self—the truth that phenomena have no intrinsic, enduring substance. Impermanence tells us that people and objects are inconstant and transitory, that thoughts and feelings are as ephemeral as foam atop a wave. Though impermanence is a reality—a natural law—we strongly resist it, for change leads to the pain and disappointment of loss. The most difficult change we face is the ultimate inescapable loss—death.

But we all know death is inevitable, don't we?

Knowing the truth and accepting it are very different things. A classic example is the story of Kisa Gotami, who could not accept that her young son had died. Clutching his lifeless body, she went from neighbor to neighbor, begging for medicine to cure him. One man took pity on her and said, "I don't have the medicine you need, but I know someone who does." When she came to me demanding the remedy, I sent her off to collect a mustard seed from every house in which no one had died. Empty-handed after a long search, she realized that death is universal, and was finally able to accept her loss. At the same time, she learned that there's a path to the deathless—to nirvana—for those who let go of their attachment to life.

Are you suggesting that liberation is possible only for those who stop caring about anything?

Letting go of attachment to life doesn't mean not caring. It means understanding that the pain of everyday experience comes from denying the truth of impermanence. When we fail to accept it, we get caught up in the vicissitudes of life, the "eight worldly conditions"—gain and loss, fame and disrepute, praise and blame, pleasure and pain—and are at the mercy of our likes and dislikes. Accepting that life is transitory lets you ease your grip on it. When you're not desperately clinging to something, you're free to care for it in a relaxed and loving way.

But if change and loss are inevitable, doesn't that make life pretty futile?

Change isn't always negative. It's the very essence of life—it's vital to growth. Without change, existence would indeed be futile: there could be no righting of wrongs, no learning, no possibility of spiritual awakening. Just as what we like inevitably changes or leaves, so too what we don't like passes. Just observe your mind at work, and you'll see this. Thoughts and feelings change constantly.

But if everything is inconstant and unreliable, what basis is there for caring? It's pretty hard to care for anything without forming some sort of attachment to it.

As you become aware that nothing lasts forever, you can deepen your appreciation for things as they are now, and not pin your hopes on what may or may not happen in the future.

But sometimes we have to think of the future. For instance, I've got this antique chair that's been in my family for generations. I'm expected to pass it on to my heirs. I can't just say, "I'll enjoy it now, and so what if it falls apart."

Is it really the chair you're holding onto? What makes it so special? The legs? The arms? The upholstery?

It's special because it's a family heirloom.

Where do you see that? Point to the "family

heirloom" part of the chair.

Don't be silly. Of course, there's no "family heirloom" part. That's just something I know.

So "family heirloom" is merely a concept, an idea you have about the chair? You're taking care of an idea?

I guess so. Put that way, it does seem a little absurd.

Whether you polish the chair every day, or give it to your nephew, or chop it up for firewood, is incidental. What you're attached to is the notion of family obligation. Apart from that, what is the chair? A nice place to sit. And just as the chair, no matter how lovingly you care for it, could disappear at any moment, your idea about it is also impermanent. What if a terrible fire reduced the chair to ash? Would you still feel the same way about it?

Of course not. It wouldn't be a chair anymore.

But aren't those ashes just the chair in another form? Do you see how readily you let go of the chair when it no longer conformed to the concept "family heirloom"? Impermanence teaches us the folly of holding onto an idea.

SELF?
THERE'S NO
SUCH THING

A common Western view of the self is that each of us is essentially a personality steering a vessel on life's waters. The vessel consists of flesh, bone, muscle, organs, a nervous system, and a brain in which memories are stored. The self—the person we are—is the captain of the ship. The Buddha, however, had a different view of self—one that may seem strangely anarchical at first, though ultimately it offers us the possibility of profound liberation.

Your view of things seems to require letting go of the notion of self altogether. Would you explain what you mean please?

We've talked about suffering and impermanence as marks of existence. The third defining mark is *anatta*—non-self. All phenomena—animate and inanimate—are without an inherent self or soul. Hindus believe in an individual soul that's eternal, transmigrating from lifetime to lifetime and eventually reuniting with the "world soul." Non-self, however, means that there's no unchanging, individuating core we can point to and say, "Here I am."

But my experience tells me there's very definitely someone sitting here now, talking to you. If this isn't my "self," what is it?

The meaning of non-self isn't that nothing exists, or that what you perceive with your senses isn't real. Conditions come together, resulting in the phenomena we experience. These phenomena exist— they just don't exist independently of the conditions that caused them.

What is a person then? Am I just the sum of all those

*traits and idiosyncrasies that make me recognizably
"me" and no one else?*

You're on the right track. A person isn't a fixed
and separate entity but a collection of physical
and mental components—*skandhas*. *Skandha* literally
means "aggregate" or "heap." There are five that
constitute a human being. One is material *form*—
the physical body, including the eyes, ears, nose,
tongue, skin, plus mind, which is considered a sense
organ in this context. From form arises *feeling*—
sensation characterized as pleasant, unpleasant, or
neutral. Then there's *perception*, which picks out
distinguishing features of experience, giving rise
to *mental formations*—emotions, volition, intention.
This is the origin of karma: we become attached
to certain mental habits and identify with them.
All this mental and physical activity gives rise to
consciousness—the experience of continuity and a
coherent self.

*So are you saying that what appears to be the captain
of the ship—the self, the ego—is just a bunch of mental
and physical sensations that come together under
certain conditions? I can't quite get my head around
this. If there isn't some essential core of self, what's
steering the ship?*

The process itself—the continual arising, fading away, and re-arising of phenomena. Reality as we know it—conditioned existence, or *samsara*—is creating itself in every moment by a chain of causality known as "dependent origination." Often that's depicted as a wheel, to indicate the cyclical nature of the twelve interconnected factors: ignorance, karma-producing formations, consciousness, mental and physical phenomena, the senses, contact with objects, feeling, craving, clinging, becoming, re-birth, and old age and death. These elements are arising in every moment, producing everything constructed, including what you call the personality or ego.

So there is no self?

The issue isn't whether there is or isn't a self, but attachment. Clinging to the notion of an enduring self leads to suffering. You're identified with the idea of "my" self and all the sensations, habits, and desires that are part of that identity. But can anything impermanent provide lasting satisfaction?

No. So how do I give up attachment to self?

Awareness. Reflect on all the ways your mind is shoring up the notion of self. Examine all the

"I wants" and "I needs"—all the likes and dislikes, all the thoughts and emotions that feed your self-concept. Be mindful of your experience as it arises. Observe it, without grasping it or labeling it "mine." As you become less self-referential, your awareness will expand.

REINCARNATION

THE
ENDLESS
TOUR

We were here before and we'll probably be here again. Getting off the reincarnation bus takes a little karma and a lot of determination. The Buddha cracked the code—discovered how to interrupt the never-ending cycle of death and rebirth. Inspired by his example, we can do the same. The present arises from the past, including past lives. The future arises from the present. To score a felicitous rebirth, we need to be mindful at all times of our thoughts, words, and actions. Especially important is our state of mind at death.

I have a lot of trouble with the idea of rebirth. How does it work?

Within the ten thousand world-systems that comprise the universe are thirty-one planes of existence onto which gods, humans, animals, and other beings are reborn as they wander through *samsara* lifetime after lifetime, until they reach nirvana and end the merry-go-round of death and rebirth. These thirty-one planes, or realms, are organized into three different worlds. The formless world contains four realms of beings who have passed beyond the physical body and exist only as consciousness in varying bliss states. The world of pure form contains sixteen different realms of *devas*, or god-like beings with bodies of pure light. Then we come to the world of the senses, with eleven different realms including the heavenly abodes of various *devas*, the human realm, the animal realm, and various hell realms. A being is reborn in a particular realm based on its karma—its volitional actions in previous lives and its state of mind at death. Human beings who behave nobly receive a fortunate rebirth in the "happy destinies"—the human or heavenly realms. Those who perform ignoble acts are reborn in the animal world or one of the hell states. Someone plagued by greed, for example, might be reborn among the hungry ghosts—beings with huge stomachs and tiny mouths who are never able to consume their fill.

Does everybody go through reincarnation?

Buddhas and some *arahats*—awakened beings—aren't reborn. After *parinirvana*—final nirvana—beings no longer incarnate. They disappear.

Then if the Buddha has disappeared, who are you? Who am I talking to?

When the Buddha's followers asked him who would teach them after his death, he told them, "Whoever sees me, sees the Dharma, and whoever sees the Dharma, sees me." You could say it isn't really the Buddha talking to you now, it's the Dharma speaking. Or, if you hold to the Mahayana view that arose in the centuries after my death, you might think of me as the Buddha manifesting in the *nirmanakaya*, or "body of transformation" that I assume to help beings reach enlightenment.

Glad you cleared that up. But what about the rest of us humans? Do we reincarnate?

So long as you're living in *samsara*—conditioned

existence—you'll be reborn. This lifetime, you were reborn as a human. That's a very propitious birth. It gives you the opportunity to awaken—to attain nirvana, the unconditioned state. Even then, according to the Mahayana tradition, you might choose the bodhisattva path and postpone *parinirvana* to remain in the human realm and help all beings awaken.

What is it that's reborn? Is there an eternal soul or self that transmigrates from one lifetime to the next?

Contrary to the *Vedas* and *Upanishads*, there's nothing to be reborn. You have no eternal soul or essential self dragging a suitcase of unresolved karma from lifetime to lifetime. Rather, what makes the trip is a continuity of consciousness at a very subtle level. Every time you generate fresh karma it leaves an energetic "stamp" on the ever-flowing mind stream. Consciousness carries these karmic stamps or "seeds" into the next incarnation, where they ripen as conditions are right. Once the karma is exhausted, it disappears from the mind stream.

I still don't see how karma from this lifetime can reappear in another lifetime without an identity attached to it.

From the perspective of consciousness, death and

rebirth are one continuum, like a river. Karma is like a wave that arises in one moment, disappears, then arises again downstream. Each wave takes a different form but all waves are made of the same water.

How does karma determine what realm a being will be reborn in?

Karma is drawn to the realm with which it resonates most, the place where it's most likely to bear fruit. That's why it's so important to purify your mind in this lifetime and take meritorious action to counter karma you've already accumulated. The state of your mind at death affects your next rebirth.

How can we ensure a favorable rebirth?

Do all you can to eliminate greed, aversion, delusion—mental afflictions that fuel the cycle of death and rebirth. Practice mindfulness meditation to know the true nature of things. Practice the Ten Perfections: generosity, morality, renunciation, wisdom, persistence, patience, truthfulness, determination, good will, and equanimity—the virtues bodhisattvas have cultivated over lifetimes to prepare for buddhahood. In short, dedicate your life to awakening.

KARMA

DO THIS, THAT HAPPENS

Karma is the natural law of moral causality that says: We reap what we sow. Positive action generally leads to happiness, negative to suffering. But does that mean, "once a scoundrel, always a scoundrel"? Not in the Buddha's view. We're the product of our past—and past lives— but the future isn't predetermined. We have the choice—and responsibility—to make of life what we will.

I'm confused about karma. It seems like some sort of cosmic justice system that rewards and punishes. Can you explain it to me please?

"Cosmic justice" implies the existence of an outside force that arbitrates human behavior. That is not the Buddha's view. Karma is simply the Pali word for "action." It's the natural law of cause and effect as it relates to ethical matters. Behavior produces results in accordance with the intention behind it. "Skillful" or positive actions are more likely to lead to desirable outcomes, unskillful or negative actions to suffering.

How, exactly, does karma work?

Your thoughts, words, and deeds plant karmic "seeds"—energy traces. When conditions are right, these seeds "ripen." Depending on the strength of your motivation and the force of the action, as well as other factors, the karmic fruits of behavior may appear immediately, or later, or even in a future lifetime. Many conditions—internal and external, past and present—affect karma. It's one of the "four unconjecturables"—it would be fruitless for you to speculate on precisely how and when it will play out. The wisest course is simply to bear in mind at all times that behavior has consequences.

So if I say something hurtful to someone, something bad will happen to me?

If you hurt someone, not only will that person suffer but so, in some way, will you. The degree of suffering will depend on many factors, some knowable, some not. If you're carrying past karma related to harmful speech—even from a previous lifetime—there may be serious repercussions. But if you're a kindly person disinclined to harsh speech, sincere apologies and remorse may be sufficient to minimize the negative karma or exhaust it on the spot.

You mentioned karma from a previous lifetime. Might temperament be the result of karma from a previous life being worked out in this one?

It might.

But if we're born with a karmic script already written for us, what can we do but make the best of it?

A fatalistic view of karma is common but illogical. It fails to take into account the reality of change. Impermanence is one of the three marks of existence. You're born with—or more accurately, because of—karma created in past lives. But by the decisions you make now, you design your own future. It's possible to mitigate the effects of past karma, as well as generate positive karma going forward.

So we have free will with respect to karma?

Volitional actions generate karma. Natural forces like the winds and tides don't. Nor do bodily functions like breathing and sleeping, or behavior that you're unaware might cause harm. Though deliberately taking a life would generate bad karma, inadvertently stepping on an ant would not. Intention is the key. Karma invites us to take responsibility for our behavior: "I am the owner of my actions, heir to my actions, born of my actions, related through my actions, and have my actions as my arbitrator. Whatever I do, for good or for evil, to that I will fall heir."

How, then, should we live in the face of karma?

Pay close attention to the quality of your thoughts, speech, and actions—above all, your intentions. Think about whether your actions might cause harm. Karma is created first in the mind. Negative karma arises from greed, anger, and ignorance—and their cousins, such as envy and pride. Action rooted in qualities like generosity and compassion produces positive karma, making life happier and more peaceful for all concerned.

What if your intentions are good but the results harmful?

There will still be karma, though it's unlikely to be as severe as that created by a selfish or destructive motivation. Karma teaches us to be mindful in every situation and make better choices.

Does karma help to explain differences between people? When two people have the same advantages, why does one become successful while the other barely scrapes by?

A successful person may be reaping the rewards of past generosity or delight in others' good fortune. Someone who's poor in this lifetime may have been miserly in a previous lifetime.

That sounds like an insidious form of determinism— blame the victim.

Too many factors give rise to karma to draw definitive conclusions. Rather than trying to determine if your current circumstances are a result of past karma working itself out, why not focus on creating a better life going forward?

DESIRE

WANTING THINGS

Pleasure, fame, praise, gain—we crave it all. Our "thirst for existence" is insatiable. Alas, an appetite for life can't guarantee happiness. In time we fall victim to our desires. Ceaselessly striving for the joys and toys of the world and trying to avoid the trials fails to bring lasting gratification. But can desire ever lead us to true happiness? The Buddha taught us it can. A longing for awakening points us toward ultimate fulfillment—an end to craving.

What's wrong with desire anyway? Isn't that what drives us to achieve?

It's true that everything that exists is born of desire. Desire brings you into the world and drives you to acquire its trappings—money, possessions, power, success. But desire is also the root of suffering. No amount of clinging can make these pleasures last. What you crave—permanence, security—you cannot have. Even the desire to avoid pain is futile. Every life is visited by sorrow. Yet, like moths to the flame, we rush toward what will ultimately destroy us—or our peace of mind, at any rate.

I'm still not clear why desire is destructive.

Tanha, desire in Pali, means thirst. And thirst can never be permanently satisfied. Acting on your desires leads to habitual ways of behaving, to automatic responses. You become entrapped in pursuing what you crave and miss out on what's genuinely important—awakening to the true nature of things.

But isn't the quest for awakening a desire in itself?

It is. The desire for nirvana—the end of desiring— is a positive desire. It makes you more persistent.

But even that desire must be abandoned eventually.

I don't understand how desire itself can put an end to desiring.

Say you want to go to the park. Don't you first have the desire to go? And then when you reach the park, don't you abandon that desire, since you've now attained your goal? So it is with the path to awakening. Motivated by the desire for liberation, you follow it diligently until you reach nirvana and freedom from desire. In certain practices of the Vajrayana—Tibetan Buddhist—tradition, desire itself is the object of meditation and the vehicle for transformation.

If desire is such a problem, why do we keep wanting?

So long as you remain in *samsara*—the cycle of death and rebirth—you're in the realm of desire. But even more than the objects of your desire, it's satisfaction you crave. However, with insight and moral discipline, over time you become disenchanted with the ceaseless pursuit of your desires. And with disenchantment, comes dispassion—detachment from sensual pleasures and worldly things. Detachment extinguishes the fires of craving.

But what brings about disenchantment? How do we stop wanting?

Think of children at the beach building sand castles. As long as they're enjoying the sand castles, they protect them. But when their interest wanes, they demolish the sand castles and walk away. Similarly, if you can mentally deconstruct the objects of your desire into their component parts, they'll no longer be objects of delight.

Are you saying that we should cut off desire by cutting off all sensory experience—denying the body and controlling the mind, in other words?

Extreme self-denial will bring you no closer to awakening than self-indulgence will. The Noble Eightfold Path to awakening is the Middle Way— the path of moderation.

What does that mean in practical terms?

The three categories of action on the path are meditation, moral discipline, and cultivation of wisdom.

Does that require us to lead a monastic life?

Not unless you choose a monastic life—or it chooses you. It's possible to walk the path of liberation while living an everyday existence. You can pursue a career, raise a family, and deal with day-to-day concerns without violating any of the precepts. What you *will* need to do, however, is make sure that your worldly ambitions don't get in the way of your spiritual goals.

As I explained to Anathapindika, a wealthy merchant who was one of my most ardent lay followers, there are four types of happiness someone living in the world can enjoy: the happiness of possession, of enjoyment, of freedom from debt, and of blamelessness.

The happiness of possession means enjoying the material success you achieve through honest striving. By "honest striving" I mean not only avoiding harmful or illegal occupations but also undertaking whatever job you do with diligence and a spirit of cooperation. The happiness of enjoyment comes from using the wealth you amass to do good—to be a contributing member of society. The happiness of being debt-free is twofold: you enjoy peace of mind from knowing you're living within your means and from being free to pursue the Dharma. The happiness of blamelessness comes from conducting yourself at all times with the utmost probity of body, speech, and mind.

So desire isn't such a dirty word after all.

Freeing yourself from desire is less about giving things up than about appreciating what you have without being attached to it. Knowing that the objects of your desire can disappear in an instant makes their enjoyment all the sweeter.

MORALITY

DO THE RIGHT THING

L eft to our own devices, we don't always make skillful choices. Knowing this, the Buddha laid out standards for an ethical life. Cultivating *sila*—virtue—promotes inner peace and right relations with the world, but moral development goes beyond good behavior. Good character is the foundation of meditation practice and the *sine qua non* of spiritual awakening. Purifying your speech, actions, and livelihood sets you on the path to liberation.

Words like "morality" and "purify" and "virtue" scare me a little. I thought Buddhism was about training the mind, not monitoring our behavior.

Morality or virtue is one of the three aspects of mental training on the Noble Eightfold Path, as well as one of the *paramitas*—qualities perfected by bodhisattvas aspiring to be buddhas. Virtue is simply a mind free of defilements—greed, hatred, and ignorance. *Sila*, the Pali word for morality or ethics, means both virtue and moral discipline. You can't develop one without the other. Virtue is both the process and the goal itself—the transformed state of mind imbued with compassion and integrity.

Where do the Five Precepts fit in?

They're recommendations for leading a virtuous life.

Why is it important to follow the precepts? Can't we rely on our consciences to steer us right?

You can, if your conscience is unfailing. For most people, that's not so. Until you've developed the all-embracing wisdom and compassion of an awakened being, you're likely to need reminding what behavior will serve the greater good and not just your desires.

Are the precepts some kind of divine law? What's the punishment if we violate them?

The precepts are not divine law, no. They're practical guidelines to help you adopt an ethical stance toward the world and behave in ways that are responsible and respectful toward all beings. Following the precepts is voluntary. Unless you violate a civil law, punishment for breaking a precept comes from an innate sense of shame or from "moral dread"—fear of censure or reprisal.

So is being virtuous primarily a social responsibility?

That's only part of it. Moral training is essential for spiritual progress, for the perfection of character that leads to awakening. Virtue is the firm foundation on which meditation practice rests. This doesn't mean you must be perfect to meditate—only that you have a clear intention to develop along moral lines.

What are the guidelines for a virtuous life?

The Noble Eightfold Path sets out three arenas of experience to consider: speech, actions, and livelihood. Right Speech means refraining from lying, gossip, and slander. Put positively, it's a commitment to truth and to using speech to unite, not divide. Not lying is the most important of the five precepts for lay people. Without truthfulness, how can people trust one another? A lie motivated by greed aims at personal gain, while an angry or malicious lie aims to hurt. Right Speech also enjoins you to refrain from "harsh speech"—abuse, insults, sarcasm—as well as idle chatter.

Would "idle chatter" include all the media noise we're subjected to—TV, Internet, text messaging, cellphones?

Be mindful of distracting input. The path of awakening is difficult enough as it is.

You mentioned "Right Action." What's that about?

That's where the rest of the five precepts come in. The first precept is: *Don't kill*. It's good to be conscientious about reverence for life, but remember that intention is the key. Accidentally stepping on an ant isn't breaking the precept. The second precept, *Don't steal*, urges you to respect others' property and not take anything you're not offered or entitled to. The third, *Abstain from sexual misconduct*, calls for responsible interpersonal relations—no adultery, sex with minors, or non-consensual sex. For monastics, this precept says no sex, period—purifying the mind calls for subduing sensory desire. The last precept proscribes the use of intoxicants.

Surely an occasional glass of wine is OK?

Whatever clouds the mind is an impediment to awakening. Even selling intoxicants goes against Right Livelihood, the third aspect of moral conduct on the Noble Eightfold Path. The point is to avoid occupations that cause harm.

I hear a lot of "avoid this" and "abstain from that."
Are there positive steps we should take to build character?

Behind unwholesome behavior we usually find grasping, ill-will, or delusion. Moral training includes cultivating their opposites: generosity, loving-kindness, and wisdom.

What's the payoff for perfecting virtue?

For one thing, you'll have no remorse. And you'll not only experience peace of mind but help to counter violence and ruthlessness in the world around you. Above all, you'll lay the foundation for the true happiness of spiritual awakening.

MINDFULNESS

ATTENTION MUST BE PAID

Practically speaking, the Buddha's teachings are about training the mind. A well-trained mind is calm, clear, and aware. It isn't pulled this way and that by desires, disturbances, or delusion. Mindfulness—attentiveness—makes every experience richer and more rewarding. When you're paying attention, you live in the here and now, not in the past or future. Meditation sharpens your focus, giving you insight into your motivations and behavior. It keeps your eyes on the ultimate prize—liberation.

Define "mindfulness" for me.

Mindfulness is attentiveness, awareness. The basis of
mindfulness is observing what's actually happening in
the mind and body at the present moment, without
judging your experience, or adding to it, or trying
to change it.

*How is that different from the way our minds usually
work?*

Unless you consciously gather your attention, your
mind is likely to be all over the place, forming ideas
and opinions, framing questions, passing judgments,
drawing conclusions—jumping from one thing
to another. There's no stability. An unstable mind
wanders off into fantasy and projection, leaving
reality behind. Mindfulness settles and concentrates
the mind, stripping away fantasy to give you a direct
experience of reality.

*But what's wrong with fantasy? Isn't that where creative
ideas come from?*

We're not talking about making art but about ideas
and perceptions that lead to wrong conclusions and,
therefore, to suffering. A common fantasy is thinking

that objects have some sort of independent, lasting existence. Mindfulness sees through the charade, revealing the truth of impermanence and the interdependence of all phenomena.

How do we develop mindfulness?

Meditation is the most powerful way to train the mind. The Pali word for meditation—*bhavana*—means mind development or cultivation. *Shamata*, or "calm abiding," is a concentration practice that brings tranquility. By staying still and focusing your attention on an object such as the breath, you develop sustained attention—one-pointedness. A mind that's calm and focused can support *vipassana*, or insight meditation—the analytical practice of observing the mind and its contents. This practice is the basis for mental mastery. Insight leads to release of the five hindrances to awakening—desire, ill-will, laziness, restlessness, and doubt—and to "clear knowing," or seeing things as they really are.

How will meditation help me handle situations in everyday life?

Meditation trains the mind to slow down and observe. It opens up an inner spaciousness in which you can watch thoughts and feelings as they arise and pass away. When you understand that moods, bodily sensations, and thoughts—however compelling— don't last, you become less reactive, reducing the likelihood of outbursts or rash behavior. A balanced mind has choices. Above all, mindfulness keeps you in the present moment. Instead of dwelling on past regrets or future speculation, you can attend fully to what's in front of you, here and now.

Imagine you notice a huge crowd of people gathered around a famous movie star. Suddenly someone hands you a bowl filled to the brim with oil and says, "You have to carry this on your head through the crowd, and if you spill a drop, we'll cut off your head." What do you think—will your attention be on the movie star or on the bowl of oil?

The oil, of course. But isn't it sometimes better not to pay attention to what's in front of you? If I'm doing something boring or routine like washing dishes or raking leaves, why shouldn't I let my mind wander and use the time productively—to ponder a problem I need to solve, say, or to hatch a creative project?

Is letting your mind wander really a productive use of your time? If you constantly chase after distant phantoms to avoid feelings of boredom or dislike, how will you ever learn to deal with the reality of displeasing mind states—or discover that acknowledging them is the first step to reducing your discomfort? When you stay in the moment mindfully, any number of things can happen. For one, you're less likely to break a dish or trip over your rake—harm yourself or others. For another, you'll finish the task faster with better results. Above all, you'll see your habitual responses clearly, giving you an opportunity to change your attitudes and behavior. Become curious about what you don't like or understand, and as you observe it, watch your feelings about it change.

Doesn't all this mindfulness inhibit spontaneity and turn us into control freaks?

Just the opposite. The more aware you are—the more fully present to your experience—the easier it becomes to react spontaneously and appropriately to whatever happens. That's very freeing. Trusting you can handle life as it arises allows you to surrender the need for control and still feel secure.

So it sounds like there are practical advantages to being mindful?

Many. Your memory and intuition will improve. You'll

become more discerning. Your body will be calm and your mind collected, free of defilements. Mindfulness helped one of my followers, King Pasenadi, curb his overeating. An attentive person knows when enough is enough. And if you practice the four foundations of mindfulness—that is, contemplating the body, feeling, mind, and mental objects for seven years or even seven days, you'll attain the knowledge of an *arahat*, or become a "non-returner," freed from rebirth in the human realm. Mindfulness is the direct path to realization of nirvana.

COMPASSION

TEA AND SYMPATHY

The Buddha radiated kindness and compassion. By his example he showed that a mind imbued with good will, courtesy, and concern for others is a liberating force. Loving-kindness, compassion, sympathetic joy, and equanimity—the *brahma-viharas*, or four "sublime abodes"—are not only vehicles for creating a harmonious life among our fellows but also the true home of an awakened heart. The Buddha taught that caring counters anger, cruelty, self-seeking, and indifference, bringing awareness and inner peace.

There's so much ill will, even hatred, in the world today. You have only to follow the news to see this. What can we do about it?

To seek happiness by hurting others is the way of the fool. As I've said, "Hatred never destroys hatred— only love does. That's the eternal law." Hatred arises when you see yourself as separate from others. When you understand your basic interconnectedness, your common humanity, positive feelings arise.

But how do we balance concern for others with the need to take care of ourselves?

The two go hand in hand. Just as no one is dearer to you than yourself, others are dear to *them*selves. If you care about yourself, you won't harm others, because you know how they feel. Harmony within yourself and with the world comes from cultivating the sublime mind states known in Pali as the *brahma-viharas*, or "four immeasurables": *metta*, loving-kindness; *karuna*, compassion; *mudita*, sympathetic joy; and *upekkha*, equanimity. *Brahma* means supreme or celestial, *vihara* means abode. These qualities are often referred to as the divine abodes—the natural dwelling places of the heart when it's free of greed, anger, aversion, and ignorance.

How do the brahma-viharas *differ from one another?*

Metta—loving-kindness—is often translated as friendliness or good will. This is brotherly love— concern for the welfare of all beings, not romantic feeling or desire. Nothing compares with the force of loving-kindness in conquering greed and ill-will. *Karuna*, or compassion, is empathy—the "trembling" of the heart in response to suffering. We bear witness to others' pain and heartache, neither turning away out of fear or disgust nor wallowing in sentimentality or excessive grief. Compassion is the antidote to cruelty. *Mudita*—sympathetic joy—is pleasure in the happiness and good fortune of others. For many people, this is the most challenging *brahma-vihara*. Out of jealousy or competitiveness, it's often easier to take comfort in someone's misfortune than to delight in their success. In cultivating sympathetic joy you overcome indifference to others.

Out of these mind states emerges *upekkha*— equanimity—the ability to stay balanced and neutral in the face of difficult people and life's vicissitudes.

Are there specific ways to develop these mind states?

One way is to send loving-kindness to all beings everywhere, wishing them safety, health, happiness, and ease of heart. I first taught the monks this practice to overcome fear. One rainy season, tree spirits were terrorizing the monks while they were on retreat in the forest. They came to me requesting another retreat spot, but I told them the only way to stop the harassment was to confront their fears. I sent them back to the forest with verses of universal love to meditate on. The monks generated so much love that the tree deities stopped bothering them and became their protectors instead.

What is the practice for cultivating loving-kindness?

As a meditation, you can send good will to all beings everywhere by repeating an aspiration such as, "May all beings be happy and secure. May their minds be contented." People nowadays usually begin this practice by repeating those phrases on their own behalf. Then you can direct loving-kindness toward a benefactor, then a dear friend, then a "neutral person"—someone for whom you have neither positive nor negative feelings. When your practice is well established, you can turn your attention to an enemy—someone with whom you're having difficulties. Finish by sending *metta* to all beings.

How can we develop compassion?

Compassion can be aroused by directing an aspiration such as "May you be free of your pain and sorrow" to the suffering person.

And sympathetic joy?

To cultivate sympathetic joy, reflect on someone's happiness or success. If the person is no longer riding high, recall a time when he was, and envision his future success. If you have difficulty being happy for someone else, reflect on your ambivalence—trace it back to its source. See that your anger, jealousy, or fear has no substance.

What about equanimity?

The traditional practice for cultivating equanimity, especially when you're upset with someone, is to reflect on the awareness that all beings are the owners of their karma and that their happiness or unhappiness depends on their own actions. Stay with this thought until both positive and negative feelings dissipate and you reach a point of no preferences. One test of your impartiality is to imagine you're walking down a road accompanied by a friend, a benefactor, a neutral person, and an enemy when a bandit suddenly accosts you, demanding that you surrender one of your party. When you truly feel that no one—including your enemy and yourself—should be sacrificed before the others, you've reached a place of equanimity.

You mentioned anger. How would the brahma-viharas *help me deal with anger toward someone—even toward a public official whose policies I vehemently oppose?*

You'd deal with it the same way. One possibility is to ignore the person. Another, to do one of the *brahma-vihara* practices we've already discussed. Sometimes just being aware that the object of your annoyance is another suffering being is enough to trigger a sense of compassion. Karma will take care of them. Your focus should be on restoring your own inner peace.

But what if the person is abusive or inconsiderate? It's hard to just ignore bad behavior or think, "Oh well, his karma will take care of him."

Look at it another way. Picture a person who's traveling along a road and suddenly becomes seriously ill, far from a hospital or assistance of any kind. Then you come along and take pity on the man, thinking, "This poor traveler needs medical attention. I'd better help, or he might succumb on the spot."

Isn't the person who annoys you just like that traveler—someone in need? He may not be physically ill, but don't you see he's in distress with all the negative karma he's accumulating? Realizing that, don't you feel a little sympathy—and hope that he'll see the error of his ways so he won't have to suffer so?

LOVE

THE PATH OF
THE HEART

Is love the answer for living well? Is there room for romance in the pursuit of enlightenment? Though the Buddha left marriage and family behind to meditate in the forest, he knew a thing or two about intimate relations. His teachings on non-harming and building trust and respect, along with the devotion he inspired in others, offer a guide to ennobling our interactions with lovers, relatives, and friends. Love, when tempered by wisdom and free of unhealthy attachment, can be a key to fulfillment.

An unfettered life may be ideal for monks, but where does that leave the rest of us who are fully involved in marriage, family, and other relationships?

I have nothing against marriage. How fortunate it is to find a suitable mate. I've only meant to suggest that from my own experience, it's easier to pursue enlightenment when you can dedicate yourself fully to the task. Work and family obligations will divert your energy and attention.

But didn't you assure your lay followers that they, too, could reach enlightenment?

I did. Anyone can walk the path to awakening. But householders also have responsibilities to family and friends. Once when we were staying in the Bamboo Grove near Rajagaha, a young disciple named Singala who was very dedicated to the Dharma asked how he should carry out his obligations to others. A true friend, I told him, is generous, sympathetic, and helpful, rejoicing in others' successes and sticking by them in difficult times. A good friend shares his secrets and keeps others' confidences. He offers wise counsel and encourages others to do their best. I also gave Singala guidelines on how husbands and wives can ensure a happy married life, and what parents and children owe another.

It seems a little strange for you to be doling out marriage and child-rearing advice when you walked out on your own wife and baby son.

My wife understood it was my karma to leave home in pursuit of spiritual awakening. In India 2,500 years ago, it wasn't unusual to renounce household life and become a wandering monk. I didn't "go forth," as it was called, without making sure my family was well cared for. If you're familiar with my life story, you know that both my wife and my son, Rahula, later became followers of the Dharma, as did many people in my extended family. The Dharma was the greatest gift, the greatest legacy, I could have offered them.

What advice do you have for husbands and wives to build a loving marriage?

It's pretty basic. A husband should cherish his wife and be faithful to her, and should be courteous and respectful, never cruel or abusive. He should give her authority over the household and be generous in fulfilling her needs. For her part, a wife should remain faithful to her husband, and should be skilled and industrious in running the home, and hospitable to relatives and visitors. She shouldn't be wasteful with her husband's money.

Some women might find that advice a little sexist, but I can see it was probably pretty revolutionary for India 2,500 years ago. Now, it's worth thinking about at least. But what about children—what should loving parents do for their kids and vice versa?

Loving parents nourish their children and protect them and "introduce them to this world," making sure they'll have a means of livelihood when they grow up and giving them their inheritance when the proper time comes. For their part, children should revere their parents and take care of them in their old age. Keeping family traditions and making charitable offerings in honor of deceased relatives are other ways children can show their love and appreciation.

You've brought love down to a very practical level. I think of it in more romantic terms. Am I missing the point?

I'm a practical man. Romance isn't love, it's infatuation—attraction that's destined to pass.

What about devotion? Isn't that love? I'm thinking of Ananda, your longtime attendant. His entire life was committed to your service.

He was a loyal friend to me and to the *sangha*, but his devotion caused him great pain as I was dying. Love in the ordinary sense involves attachment. And with attachment comes the pain of change, separation, and loss. Remember our conversation about the *brahma-viharas*, the sublime mind states? The love associated with loving-kindness, compassion, sympathetic joy, and equanimity doesn't involve clinging to an object or a state of mind and is therefore free of the suffering that comes with attachment.

I'm confused. Earlier you said there was nothing wrong with marriage. But the love between two people in a committed relationship is bound to involve attachment and therefore, according to what you're now saying, suffering. So I guess romantic love has no place on the path to awakening.

The virtues of true friendship—generosity, kind words, mutual support, consistent presence—make it a worthy, even noble endeavor. Though some degree of attachment is inevitable in an intimate connection, it isn't necessarily unwholesome attachment. Through attachment you learn about non-attachment—not clinging. Every relationship, intimate or friendly, can be a way for two people to grow in the Dharma. Each is a mirror for the other, reflecting any character flaws that need correcting, any residue of possessiveness, anger, or self-preoccupation. Love can be the path to enlightenment. Just don't expect *romantic* love to do it for you.

THE BODY

LOTUS TIME

Sex. Post-enlightenment, the Buddha wasn't having any. To his early followers, the body was something of an inconvenience. Later, Tibetan Buddhists embraced it as an "abode of bliss" fostering sacred union. Instead of a "bag of filth" to be "endured with equanimity," the body was acknowledged as a vehicle of liberation. Some scholars even say the Buddha attained nirvana not under the bodhi tree but during a tantric ritual with his wife. An arguable claim. Still, whatever it *isn't*, the body is the seat of meditation.

You've referred to the body as "sick, putrid, unclean,"
"a heap of festering wounds," "a nest of diseases."
What have you got against it?

The body itself isn't the problem. It's just a bag of
bones and tissue and fluids that sickens, ages, and
dies. The problem is attachment—fascination with
the body and the sensory desires that arise in it.

But your teachings include a giant plug for celibacy.
If that's not denial of the body, what is?

I teach only the truth of suffering and how to end
suffering. Nirvana means freedom from desire.
Sensual desire is the first of the five hindrances—
negative mind states that block the way to awakening.
In one of my first addresses, now known as the Fire
Sermon, I said, "All is burning. And what, monks, is
the all that is burning? The eye … the ear … the nose
… the tongue … the body … the mind … Burning
with what? With the fire of lust, with the fire of
hatred, with the fire of delusion … " There are many
sensual desires humans are prey to, but hunger for
sex is one of the most insistent. To achieve inner
freedom, lust must be subdued. Therefore, celibacy
is a basic rule of monastic life—monks who break
this vow are expelled. Celibacy is essential not only

to facilitate individual awakening but also to maintain order within the community.

What happened to the Middle Way? I thought the Eight-fold Path was supposed to be a moderate course between the extremes of licentiousness and rigid self-denial?

The precepts for lay people don't say, "no sex." The third precept says, "I will not engage in sexual misconduct." Broadly, sexual misconduct means exploitive or non-consensual sex—anything from rape to adultery to a sex act your partner doesn't willingly agree to.

In the Fire Sermon, you said that "when the fire of lust is extinguished, one is liberated." You were referring to all sensual desires, not just sex. But how are we supposed to extinguish sexual desire?

There are various methods of working with the mind to subdue sexual desire. By meditating on unpleasant objects you withdraw your attention from the objects of your desire, becoming "disenchanted" with the body. One practice involves reflecting on the "foulness" of the body, examining in turn each body part and all the various fluids and secretions. Another practice consists of contemplating the body as a corpse lying in a cemetery or charnel ground, being picked to the bone by vultures and hyenas. When you see the body as a corpse or a "heap of festering wounds," your infatuation with it dissipates.

You can't tell me you don't think of sex now and then— when you catch sight of a beautiful woman, for example.

Once I attained enlightenment, sexual desire ceased altogether.

It seems that not all your followers think it's possible to get rid of sexual desire by meditating on the body's bad points, as you've described. Don't some Buddhists believe that embracing our desires, not renouncing them, is the path to awakening?

I presume you're referring to the tantra teachings of the Vajrayana, or "Diamond Vehicle." Tibetan Buddhists believe I passed along these teachings while in my *dharmakaya* body—my transcendent manifestation. Instead of repressing or sublimating sexual desire through celibacy, tantric practitioners actively engage it as a tool for liberation. Sometimes this is through ritualized sex with a tantric partner but more often through visualization of male and female deities engaged in coitus, symbolizing the union of feminine wisdom energy and the masculine energy of compassion.

This sounds rather complicated. Can anyone follow the tantric path?

Tantra is for passionate people, it's often said. Practitioners use their passion—including the intense energy of sexual desire—to open the heart and purify the mind. From this, bliss arises.

So rather than being eliminated, sensual pleasure is transmuted into spiritual ecstasy?

Something like that, although ecstasy is not the goal, awakening is. Bear in mind that tantric practice is not ordinary sex. Teachings involving sexual yoga are understandably considered "secret" or esoteric, transmitted only by adept masters to students who have undergone extensive meditation training in preparation.

The idea behind tantra is that sexual energy isn't going to just vanish, however hard you meditate. To the Vajrayana way of thinking, it's only through fully experiencing desire that you can master it and become enlightened in this lifetime.

THE WAY OF THE BODHISATTVA

AFTER YOU!

Seeking liberation is a noble goal, the path of the *arahat*, or "worthy one," trod by the Buddha's early followers. However, the *bodhisattva*, or "enlightenment being," aspires to something more—enlightenment not just for oneself but for the good of all. In the Mahayana view, we're all buddhas, already awakened—we just don't know it yet. Inspired by the Buddha's journey of self-liberation—and his infinite compassion and wisdom—the bodhisattva vows to guide us toward freedom and realization of our buddha-nature.

*In your day, the highest aspiration was to be an arahat.
Now, it seems, nobody's content with that. Everybody
wants to be a buddha. In fact, some teachers tell us we
already are buddhas but don't realize it because our minds
are still clouded by greed, aversion, and delusion.*

That's the Mahayana view, that everyone has buddha-
nature—buddha-potential waiting to be actualized.
As you say, early followers of the Dharma strove
to become *arahats*—to be liberated from *samsara*
and escape rebirth in the human realm. When the
Mahayana tradition unfolded in the centuries after
my death, its adherents held that it was selfish to
pursue enlightenment strictly for oneself. But it was
out of compassion for the suffering of the world that
I decided to pass on the truths I'd learned, and it was
out of compassion that I sent my first sixty followers
off to teach the Dharma to others. After my time, the
Mahayana developed the way of the *bodhisattva*, or
"enlightenment being," to its fullest. The bodhisattva
helps others become enlightened. This is best
accomplished by being fully awakened, with the
purified mind of a buddha. The bodhisattva vows to
withhold *parinirvana*—final enlightenment—until
all beings everywhere are liberated.

Whose idea was it—the way of the bodhisattva?

The term "bodhisattva" originally referred to me in the days—and lifetimes—before my enlightenment. It has since been applied to anyone aspiring to be a buddha. My infinite compassion toward all beings serves as the model for the bodhisattva's altruistic dedication.

Are there bodhisattvas around now?

Undoubtedly. In the Mahayana view, there are bodhisattvas on the earthly plane working toward perfection of the *paramitas*, or virtues of a buddha, while transcendent bodhisattvas, who've already reached perfection, are hovering in the heavenly realms to help worldlings in their spiritual aspiration. The most revered of the transcendent bodhisattvas is Avalokitesvara, the bodhisattva of compassion. Known as Chenrezig to Tibetan Buddhists, Kannon to the Japanese, and Kwan Um to Koreans, he has a female counterpart in the Chinese bodhisattva Kuan Yin.

How is it decided who'll become a bodhisattva? Is the path open to anyone?

Karma nudges some people toward the path of liberation. Then they must arouse *bodhicitta*, or "enlightenment heart-mind"—the altruistic wish to awaken for the benefit and liberation of all beings. *Bodhicitta* is more than a feeling of compassion—the bodhisattva actively assumes responsibility for others' well-being. This ideal is reflected in the Bodhisattva's Vow, which says, in short:

However innumerable all beings are,
  I vow to save them all.
However inexhaustible delusions are,
  I vow to extinguish them all.
However immeasurable Dharma teachings are,
  I vow to master them all.
However endless the Buddha's Way is,
  I vow to follow it.

Let's say I've aroused bodhicitta *and taken the Bodhisattva's Vow. What's next?*

Cultivating the *paramitas*, the perfections. The original list sets out the ten virtues I perfected over many lifetimes in preparation for my final rebirth and awakening as Shakyamuni Buddha: generosity, morality, renunciation, wisdom, persistence, patience, truthfulness, determination, good will, and equanimity. The Mahayana revised the list. The Prajnaparamita, or Perfection of Wisdom Sutra, cites six perfections: generosity, morality, patience,

effort, meditation, and wisdom. A later Mahayana
sutra adds another four: skillful means, determination,
spiritual power, and knowledge. Together, these
virtues correspond to the *bhumis*—the ten "lands"
or stages of spiritual attainment on the path to
buddhahood.

*Whoa. I thought you said the way of the bodhisattva
was open to anyone, but all these stages and virtues are
a little overwhelming. Isn't there a beginner's course?*

Why not just start where I did as a bodhisattva—
with practicing the perfection of generosity? To give
when you're asked is good; to give *before* you're asked
is even better. Best of all is to give the very best of
what you have.

*Is all this self-sacrifice necessary? How can giving up
my life for others really help them?*

You're not giving up your life for others—you're
dedicating it to their welfare. A bodhisattva pledges
to relieve suffering wherever possible. The way to
do that is by perfecting yourself—by practicing the
paramitas and developing the qualities of a buddha.
To that end, generosity is for your own benefit,
releasing you from greed and desire.

INTERDEPENDENCE

GOOD
NEIGHBORS

We're in this together, the Avatamsaka Sutra tells us. Each person is a jewel reflecting every other jewel in the god Indra's vast celestial net. Social injustice, economic inequality, political oppression—violence to any one of us does violence to us all, the Buddha said. Wisdom and compassion, his teachings tell us, are our best weapons against threats to our safety and happiness, while generosity is essential to ensure material stability for everyone—a precondition for spiritual attainment and social harmony.

*Buddhist practice emphasizes an inner-focused spiritual
life. How do we reconcile that with the kind of action
needed to deal with violence and injustice in the world?*

Do you see a distinction between spiritual practice
and action in the world? The teaching of *paticca-
samuppada*, or dependent origination, tells us that
nothing in the world exists in isolation. The outer
environment is a reflection of your inner life. Conflict
on a broad scale arises out of self-centeredness,
intolerance, and a sense of separation in the hearts
and minds of individuals.

*But so much of the violence—war, at any rate—seems to
be precipitated by our leaders. What can we as individuals
do about it?*

You can only escape violence by removing its causes
from your own heart. Meditation practice is a force
for peace. Loving-kindness meditation, as we've
discussed, is one way to break down the sense of
separateness that prevents you from identifying with
the plight of others. Another way is a practice devised
by the Tibetan Buddhists long after my time. Called
tonglen—giving and taking—it opens your heart to
all who suffer and connects you to your natural core
of goodness, so you can transmute anger and despair

into loving-kindness and send it to others. It helps if you first practice *tonglen* in behalf of someone you care about before addressing a person or group you see as an enemy.

Begin by sitting quietly and letting the mind come to rest. Then visualize the person who's suffering, imagining in detail every aspect of their distress. When you have a deep sense of their rage or anguish, visualize it as a dense, dark ball of smoke. Inhale, drawing the smoke deep within you, then imagine it being cleansed of all negativity and transformed into pure white light. As you exhale, send the light of peace to the suffering person.

A lot of the conflict today seems to be caused by economic disparity. How do we deal with that?

Economic iniquity arises from minds tainted with greed and envy born of a sense of lack. Generosity can erode the disparity between rich and poor. When you understand that distinctions between human beings are baseless, a desire to ease the suffering of others naturally arises.

In my day, the caste system in India was very strong. Those who sought the Dharma came from every walk of life, and at times there was dissension in the *sangha*. The teachings, however, are clear: the

Dharma is the same for all, and all are one in the eyes of the Dharma.

Didn't quarrels break out on occasion, with sangha members storming off in a huff? Weren't there even threats on your life?

There were people who disagreed with the teachings. Some who left came back. A few did not. Threats to the safety and well-being of the community weren't tolerated. Those who were disruptive were asked to leave. The Dharma—and indeed monkhood—are for those who seek it sincerely. Not everyone is cut out to live a life of strict renunciation, but the Dharma is available to all. It does not discriminate.

Is violence ever justified? What about defending ourselves? Is there such a thing as a just war?

No, no, and no. As I've said often, hatred never appeases hatred. Only love does. When someone is angry, your best defense is to "mindfully grow calm." The person who doesn't lose his temper at someone who's angry "wins a battle hard to win."

Are you suggesting it's OK if the person who attacks you gets away with your property and maybe even your life,

and a despot continues to torture and torment his
subjects? Surely well-placed anger—and, if necessary,
force—are not only acceptable but our duty to our
fellows in such circumstances.

Happy is the person who can live without hatred
among hate-filled people. The hardest thing in the
world to do is exercise restraint in the face of rage,
but meeting anger with anger only makes things
worse. Sometimes self-protection is necessary, but
whenever possible, "moral strength" is preferable
to physical might. As for "just" war, there's no such
thing. "Victory begets enmity; the defeated dwell
in pain." The party who wins feels superior, which
creates more anger and distress in the defeated.
When there's no battle, there's no issue over
victory or defeat.

*Are you saying that competition of any kind goes against
the Dharma?*

Wherever there's gain and loss, envy can arise.
Inequality breeds hatred and unrest. The path to
happiness lies not in emphasizing the differences
between people but in recognizing the similarities.
Humanity's survival depends on peaceful coexistence,
not just with each other but also with the natural

world. A truly ethical life is built on tolerance, compassion, and a sense of responsibility for the welfare of all.

Is anger ever positive?

Anger is a destructive emotion, not to be indulged. Speak harshly and the words may be tossed back at you. Like a creeper vine that strangles the tree on which it grows, when you give in to anger, you harm yourself—and your enemy wins. Rather than acting or speaking in anger, the skillful response is to find a way to open your heart. Then you can take constructive action without adding to the violence in the world.

NOTES

Abbreviations for Pali texts:
DN   Digha Nikaya
MN   Majjhima Nikaya
SN   Samyutta Nikaya
AN   Anguttara Nikaya
Dmp Dhammapada
Sn   Sutta Nipata

Source: accesstoinsight.org, unless indicated

p.11 "I am born ..." E.H. Johnson, *Buddhacarita*, p.4
p.11 "This one ... all" Sn 3:2
p.12 "I lived ... dew" AN 3:38
p.13 "The murderer ... pleasure" *Buddhacarita*, iii.30, p.37
p.13 "How can I ..." *Buddhacarita*, iii.37, p.38
p.13 "... suffering" SN 12:65
p.13 "A man ..." T.W. Rhys Davids (trans.), *Buddhist Birth-Stories and Nidana-Katha* (AES, 1999), p.167
p.14 "... homelessness" MN 36, *Life of the Buddha*, p.10
p.16 "... sublime peace" MN 26

p.16 "like time ..." *Vision of the Buddha*, p.15
p.17 "grueling ..." MN 36
pp.16–17 His mind ... awakening MN 36
p.17 "given up ..." MN 36 *Life of the Buddha*, p.41
p.18 "Desire ..." Sn 3:2
p.18 "purpose ..." *Buddhacarita*, xiii.66, p.200
p.19 "aging-less ..." MN 26, *In the Buddha's Words*, p.70
p.20 "drowning ..." SN 6:1
p.21 "Go now ... in the end" *Life of the Buddha*, p.52
p.23 "Any material ..." / Practice ... blessings MN 62, *Life of the Buddha*, pp.122–3
p.26 "All conditioned ..." SN 6:15, *Buddhism: The Illustrated Guide*, p.41
p.26 "Be islands ..." DN 16
p.26 "He who sees ..." SN 22:87 *Life of the Buddha*, p.197
p.27 "... practice" AN 3:65
p.33 Four Noble Truths Bhikkhu Bodhi, *The Nobility of the Truths*; Thanissaro

Bhikkhu, *The Four Noble Truths* (accesstoinsight.org)

p.37 Eightfold Path Bhikkhu Bodhi, *The Noble Eightfold Path* (Pariyatti, 2000); *What the Buddha Taught*

p.41 impermanence Bhikkhu Bodhi, *Anicca Vata Sankhara*; Thanissaro Bhikkhu, *All About Change* (accesstoinsight.org)

p.46 non-self Thanissaro Bhikkhu, *The Not-self Strategy* (accesstoinsight.org); David J. Kalupahana, *The Principles of Buddhist Psychology* (SUNY Press, 1987), pp.17–27

p.50 suffering *Foundations of Mindfulness*, pp.112–19; Thanissaro Bhikkhu, *Questions of Skill* (accesstoinsight.org); Bhikkhu Bodhi, *Does Rebirth Make Sense?* (accesstoinsight.org); *The Thirty-one Planes of Existence* (accesstoinsight.org)

p.58 karma Thanissaro Bhikkhu, *Kamma and the Ending of Kamma*; Nyanatiloka Mahathera, *Karma and Rebirth* (accesstoinsight.org)

p.60 "unconjecturables" AN 4:77

p.62 "I am ... heir" AN 5:57

p.74 developing virtue Bhikkhu Bodhi, *Nourishing the Roots* (accesstoinsight.org)

p.75 Moral training Ajahn Lee Dhammadharo, *The Craft of the Heart, Part I: Mastering Virtue,* trans. Thanissaro Bhikkhu (accesstoinsight.org)

p.88 "Hatred ..." Dmp 5

p.88 brahma-viharas Sharon Salzberg, *Loving-kindness: The Revolutionary Art of Happiness* (Shambhala, 1995)

p.99 "introduce ..." AN 2:31–32

p.104 "sick ... diseases" *Therigatha* 5:4, Dmp 147

p.104 "All is burning ..." SN 35:29, *Buddha's Words*, p.346

p.119 "mindfully ... /... win" SN 7:2

p.120 "moral strength" Elizabeth Harris, *Violence and Disruption in Society: A Study of the Early Buddhist Texts* (accesstoinsight.org)

p.120 "Victory ..." Dmp 201

FURTHER RESEARCH

BOOKS

Karen Armstrong, *Buddha* (Penguin, 2004)

Sir Edward Arnold, *The Light of Asia* (www.buddhanet.net)

Bhikkhu Bodhi, *In the Buddha's Words* (Wisdom, 2005)

Rupert Gethin, *The Foundations of Buddhism* (Oxford/Opus, 1998)

Ven. Henepola Gunarata, *Mindfulness in Plain English* (Wisdom, 1991)

E.H. Johnson, *Asvaghosa's Buddhacarita or Acts of the Buddha* (Motilal Banasidass, 1984)

Jack Kornfield and Gil Fronsdal (trans.), *The Dhammapada: A New Translation of the Buddhist Classic* (Shambhala, 2005)

Tom Lowenstein, *The Vision of the Buddha* (Duncan Baird Publishers/Barnes & Noble, 2005)

Bhkkhu Nanamoli, *The Life of the Buddha* (Pariyatti, 2001)

Thich Nhat Hanh, *Old Path White Clouds* (Parallax Press, 1991)

Walpola Rahula, *What the Buddha Taught* (Grove Press, 1974)

Dr. Osamu Tezuka, *Buddha*, manga (comics) 8 vols. (Vertical Books, 2003–5)

Kevin Trainor (ed.), *Buddhism: The Illustrated Guide* (Duncan Baird Publishers, 2001)

PERIODICALS

Buddhadharma: The Practioner's Quarterly
www.thebuddhadharma.com

Shambhala Sun
www.shambhalasun.com

Tricycle: The Buddhist Review
www.tricycle.com

WEBSITES

Access to Insight
www.accesstoinsight.org

BuddhaNet www.buddhanet.net

Buddhist Studies Virtual Library www.ciolek.com/WWWVL-Buddhism.html

DharmaNet International
www.dharmanet.org

INDEX